ON A
CAR JOURNEY
IN FRANCE

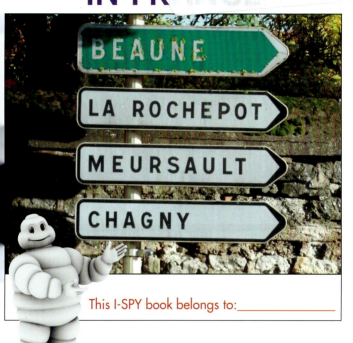

BEAUNE

LA ROCHEPOT

MEURSAULT

CHAGNY

This I-SPY book belongs to:_____

I-SPY

Introduction

The populations of France and the United Kingdom are similar but in terms of land area, France is more than twice as big. By British standards, therefore, France is a very rural country. And, once you are out of the larger towns and cities, this is the impression you have as you drive along kilometre after kilometre of arrow-straight, tree-lined roads bordered by hectares of maize or sunflowers. Bounded by three seas, the English Channel, the Atlantic, and the Mediterranean in the south, France is a country of variety, and, at the same time, one of strong national identity. As a nation, France is proud of its language, its culture, and its heritage, but its people remain as individual as any in the world. For these reasons, any visitor to the country will instantly recognize its Frenchness but, at the same time, the variety and individuality provide an ideal opportunity for I-Spy.

In the south, the French Riviera is a region of golden beaches where the rich and famous bask under the hot Mediterranean sun. In the north, in Normandy, where a more 'English' climate prevails, dairy farming and apple orchards abound. There are the mountains of the Auvergne and the Massif Central; to the south, France

and Spain are separated by the mighty Pyrenees; and to the south-east, the Alps provide a spectacular divide between France and Switzerland.

Prehistoric caves, Roman ruins, medieval towns with cobbled streets, chateaux large and small, and the most romantic and stylish of cities, Paris, all contrive to add interest to a land rich in elegance and beauty. As well as the delights of its landscape and the uniqueness of its people, there are two more features of France which serve indelibly to identify the country: its cuisine and its wines. Both have been exported to the furthest-flung outposts of the world. But both continue to play a vital role in the everyday life of France and the French. With so many places to visit and so much of interest to see, I-Spy On a Car Journey in France offers a tempting taste of the country's wealth of fascinating features. To make the most of your journey in France, use Michelin's extensive range of maps and guides.

How to use your I-SPY book

You need 1000 points to send off for your I-Spy badge (see P64) but that is not too difficult because there

are masses of points in every book. As you make each I-Spy, write your score in the box and, where

there is a question, double your score if you can answer it.

One of the first things a visitor to France will notice is the variety of French Road signs. In many ways, apart from the language differences, the road signs are similar to British signs. In Britain, many drivers use road numbers to navigate from one place to another. French drivers, however, prefer to use place names as a guide, and, in many cases, major place names beyond the driver's destination are used for navigation.

BLUE SIGNS

The blue signs indicate the way to an important destination, and the route to the motorway.

I - SPY points: 5

BORDER

Drivers approaching the French border will see a sign informing them that the border is ahead.

I - SPY points: 20

MOTORWAY AHEAD

This blue sign lets you know that the motorway is ahead.

I - SPY points: 5

GREEN SIGNS

This collection of signs, located in the town, points the way to the motorways.

I - SPY points: 10

3

PASS EITHER SIDE

This green and white sign is found at the apex of slip road junctions.

 I - SPY points: 5

MOTORWAY

If you see one of these, you are now on the motorway!

 I - SPY points: 5

MULTIPLE SIGNS

Here is a sign with multiple destinations and route options.

 I - SPY points: 10

WEATHER RESTRICTOR

The speed limit on French motorways varies depending on weather conditions. 130km/h in good weather, 110km/h when it is raining.

 I - SPY points: 10

SERVICES AHEAD
Services 1500m ahead.

 I - SPY points: 10

PEAGE
A road toll is required when travelling on some major French roads. Vehicles are waiting here to make a payment at a peage station.

 I - SPY points: 10

EXITS
Exits ahead!

I - SPY points: 5

END OF THE MOTORWAY
You have reached the end of the motorway and normal speed limits and regulations apply.

 I - SPY points: 10

ONE WAY

An arrow to indicate the direction of flow.

 I - SPY points: 5

CHEVRON ARROWS

You will see these arrows on a bend or roundabout.

 I - SPY points: 10

ROUNDABOUT

Roundabouts mainly operate the same way in France as in Britain – except you must go around anti-clockwise! .

 I - SPY points: 5

NO OVERTAKING

I - SPY points: 5

GIVE WAY

I - SPY points: 5

CHANNEL TUNNEL

Here is a sign to the 'tunnel under the channel'.

I - SPY points: 15

RURAL DIRECTIONS

This signpost gives directions to a major destination and three white signs for local towns or villages.

I - SPY points: 5, for each of the green and white signs

STOP – NO ENTRY

 I - SPY points: 5

Roundabout
Approaching a roundabout,
you must give way to the traffic
already on the roundabout.

 I - SPY points: 5

NO LEFT TURN

 I - SPY points: 5

NO RIGHT TURN

 I - SPY points: 5

STOP

This English word is universally known!

 I - SPY points: 5

NO WAITING

 I - SPY points: 5

NO U-TURN

 I - SPY points: 5

SCHOOL AHEAD

 I - SPY points: 5

Here are some other road signs you may see.

I - SPY points: 5, for each

GRADIENT DOWNHILL

NO ENTRY EXCEPT FOR FARM VEHICLES

PEDESTRIAN CROSSING

HEIGHT AND WIDTH RESTRICTIONS

KILOMETRE POST INDICATING THE ROAD NUMBER

TRAFFIC PRIORITY

Just like in Britain, France has various speed limited which must be obeyed. Here are a few to spot. Remember they are in kilometres per hour.

70 KM/H

 I - SPY points: 5

90 KM/H

I - SPY points: 5

110 KM/H

 I - SPY points: 5

END OF LIMIT

 I - SPY points: 5

DETOUR

The road is closed and there is a detour.

 I - SPY points: 10

PASS ON BOTH SIDES

 I - SPY points: 10

ROAD NARROWS IN BOTH LANES

 I - SPY points: 10

MEN AT WORK

I - SPY points: 5

CROSS TO OTHER SIDE

I - SPY points: 10

USE OTHER FOOTPATH

I - SPY points: 10

As you enter a French town, there are always signs to help you.

TOURIST ATTRACTION

This sign indicates that the village has a tourist attraction.

 I - SPY points: 15

TWINNING

This town is twinned with places in Germany, Britain and Belgium.

 I - SPY points: 15

ENTERING A TOWN

This is the sign you will see on entering a town or village…

 I - SPY points: 10

LEAVING A TOWN

…and this one when leaving it.

I - SPY points: 10

CHILDREN MUST HOLD AN ADULT'S HAND

I - SPY points: 15

LEVEL CROSSING

I - SPY points: 5

LEVEL CROSSING – GUARDED

I - SPY points: 10

LEVEL CROSSING – UNGUARDED

Be careful!

I - SPY points: 10

TAXI LINE

If you need a taxi, it is best to join a taxi line outside the train station or a hotel.

 I - SPY points: 10

PARKING

Motorcycles and bicycles need somewhere to park too!

 I - SPY points: 10

SPACE INDICATOR

As you approach a town or city, it's a good idea to find out where the car parking spaces are. These signs are a good way to find a space.

 I - SPY points: 10

PARKING

Parking in towns and cities can be difficult. Look for one of the municipal car parks.

 I - SPY points: 5

FLAGS

Can be found outside Hôtel de Ville and other public buildings.

I - SPY points: 10 for each flag, 5 points for other flags

EUROPEAN UNION ◯

FRANCE ◯

ITALY ◯

UNITED KINGDOM ◯

LEARNER DRIVER

This auto école car is being used by a learner driver.

 I - SPY points: 15

PROVISIONAL DRIVER

The A sign in the window indicates that this is a newly qualified driver.

 I - SPY points: 15

CITROËN TRACTION AVANT

This Citroën is a symbol of an earlier France. At the time, it was revolutionary as the first mass produced front wheel drive car.

 I - SPY points: 40

CITROËN H VAN

This old Citroën van was also very popular. They are harder to find on the roads these days.

 I - SPY points: 35

CITROËN 2CV

A symbol of France. The Citroën 2CV or Deux-Chevaux is still extremely well loved, even though they are no longer manufactured.

 I - SPY points: 10

CITROËN DS

The Citroën DS is another French classic car.

 I - SPY points: 25

2CV VAN

This 2CV is a multipurpose van…

 I - SPY points: 15

HAND PAINTED

…and this once has been hand painted! 2CV means 'two horses'.

 I - SPY points: 20

As France is a rural country, with vast areas of land, many animals can be found all over the countryside.

PIG

I - SPY points: 10

COCKEREL

I - SPY points: 10

HORSE

I - SPY points: 10

SHEEP

I - SPY points: 10

DUCKS

 I - SPY points: 5

GOAT

 I - SPY points: 10

COW

I - SPY points: 10

HAY BALES

 I - SPY points: 10

In the summer months, The French countryside comes alive with colour.
Here are some examples of what you may see.

GRAPES

 I - SPY points: 15

LAVENDER

I - SPY points: 10

SUNFLOWERS

 I - SPY points: 10

POPPIES

 I - SPY points: 10

VINEYARDS

I - SPY points: 15

WHEAT

I - SPY points: 10

TRACTOR

I - SPY points: 10

WELL

I - SPY points: 15

23

Camping is very popular in France and many people take their holidays on the many campsites all over the county.

OLD CITROËN VAN

This old Citroën H van has been lovingly restored and converted into a camper van.

 I - SPY points: 35

CAMPSITE SIGN

You will need to find your way to the campsite.

 I - SPY points: 10

TENT

An easy way to earn some points on a campsite!

 I - SPY points: 5

CARAVAN

A more comfortable way to camp, take your home on wheels with you!

 I - SPY points: 10

BEWARE OF CYCLISTS

 I - SPY points: 15

GREEN ROUTE

This route designated for cyclists and walkers.

 I - SPY points: 15

CYCLE WAY

This road sign indicates a cycle path.

 I - SPY points: 15

HIRE BIKES

Like London, Paris has introduced a successful bikes-for-hire system. A great way to see Paris.

 I - SPY points: 10

At the Shops

Here are a selection of shops that you may find in France. France is famous for its excellent selection of home grown produce.

BUTCHER

 I - SPY points: 10

FLORIST

 I - SPY points: 10

FRUIT AND VEGETABLE STALL

 I - SPY points: 10

FISHMONGER

 I - SPY points: 15

MARKET

I - SPY points: 10

GARDEN CENTRE

I - SPY points: 15

CHOCOLATE SHOP

I - SPY points: 20

BAKER

I - SPY points: 10

TYRE REPAIR

I - SPY points: 10

WINE SHOP

I - SPY points: 15

LOCAL GARAGE

I - SPY points: 20

CHEMIST

I - SPY points: 10

France has many regional banks but you will find branches of these national banks all over the country.

I - SPY points: 10, for each

CRÉDIT AGRICOLE

◯

SOCIÉTÉ GÉNÉRALE

◯

CAISSE D'EPARGNE

◯

CRÉDIT MUTUEL

◯

BANQUE POPULAIRE

◯

BNP PARIBAS

◯

TRAIN STATION

Most towns have a train station. This is a picture of the Eurostar station at Lille.

 I - SPY points: 10, for a train station, double for one with Eurostar

METRO

It is not only Paris that operates an underground or metro railway system. Other French cities have them too.

 I - SPY points: 25, for a non-Paris Metro

TRAIN STATION SIGN

This is a train station sign in a provincial town.

 I - SPY points: 15

INFORMATION BOOTH

You may need to ask for help or information regarding your journey.

 I - SPY points: 15

Here are some of the trains that you may find during your travels in France.

LOCAL TRAINS

Local commuter trains often have an upper deck, like a double-decker bus on their busy routes.

 I - SPY points: 15

TGV

This is the most prestigious train in France, the TGV, which stands for Train à Grande Vitesse (high-speed train) and can travel over 300kph (186mph).

 I - SPY points: 20

EUROSTAR

The Eurostar runs from stations in Paris and Belgium, through the channel tunnel and onto London. You may have started your journey on one!

 I - SPY points: 15, double if you travelled in one

Situated along the River Seine, Paris is the capital of the republic in every sense. Though, geographically, the city is located towards the north of France, it maintains its status as the physical hub of the country in that the major transport routes radiate outwards like the spokes of a wheel.

EIFFEL TOWER

The Eiffel Tower, built 'temporarily' for the Paris exhibition in 1889, reaches a height of 300m (984ft) and fortunately it still exists today.

 I - SPY points: 5

GUSTAVE EIFFEL

At the foot of one of the tower's legs is a bust of the Eiffel Tower's builder, the engineer and designer, Alexandre Gustave Eiffel (1832-1923).

 I - SPY points: 15

THE LOUVRE

Famous for da Vinci's priceless Mona Lisa, with her enigmatic smile, the Louvre houses France's most famous art collection.

 I - SPY points: 10

LOUVRE PYRAMID

France is renowned for its adventurous and avant-garde architecture. Beside the Louvre is a pyramid in glass, surrounded by water spouts, which thrust from the concrete to give access to the gallery beneath.

 I - SPY points: 10

NOTRE DAME

Cathédrale Notre-Dame, built during the twelfth and thirteenth centuries, was restored during the 1800s and made famous by Victor Hugo's novel *The Hunchback of Notre-Dame* written in 1831.

 I - SPY points: 10

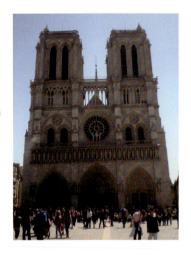

ARC DE TRIOMPHE

At the end of the Champs-Élysées, stands the magnificent Arc de Triomphe built in 1836 to commemorate Napoleon's victories. Beneath the arch is the eternal flame marking the site where an unknown soldier from World War I was buried in 1920.

 I - SPY points: 10

SACRÉ-CŒUR

Built in 1876 on Paris's most prominent hilltop, Sacré-Cœur Basilica marks the site where a popular uprising was bloodily repressed in 1871.

 I - SPY points: 10

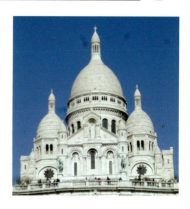

MONTMARTRE

Close to Sacré-Cœur, also on the hill, is Montmartre, still a favourite haunt of painters, sculptors, and musicians who gather on the famous square, La Place du Tertre.

 I - SPY points: 15

MOULIN ROUGE

Built in 1889 and home of the famous Can-Can dance.

 I - SPY points: 15

POMPIDOU CENTRE

Centre Georges Pompidou, known also as Beaubourg, is another centre for the arts. Pompidou (1911-74) was a French statesman and patron of the arts who succeeded de Gaulle as President of the Republic in 1969.

 I - SPY points: 15

STREET ENTERTAINERS

Outside the Pompidou Centre, there is usually a myriad of often-colourful street entertainers.

 I - SPY points: 10

BATEAU MOUCHE

A Bateau Mouche, showing passengers the delights of Paris. A wonderful way way to enjoy the city sights.

 I - SPY points: 15

METRO

These elaborate entrances to the Paris Metro – the underground railway – were designed by Hector Guimard (1867-1942), the French Art Nouveau architect.

 I - SPY points: 5

LES INVALIDES

Today, Les Invalides holds the tombs of France's military heroes, including Napoleon I and Foch, as well as the Musée de l'Armée. It was originally built by Louis XIV as a home for disabled soldiers and has a gold leafed dome.

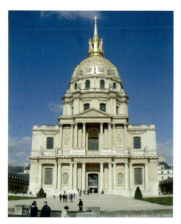

 I - SPY points: 15

POST BOX

The familiar yellow post box of France.

 I - SPY points: 10

POSTMAN WITH HIS BICYCLE

You may have to be up early in the morning to spot one!

 I - SPY points: 15

POST OFFICE

La Poste is the national postal service of France. Here is a post office.

 I - SPY points: 5

POST VAN

In its yellow and blue livery, a modern La Poste van is unmistakeable.

 I - SPY points: 10

VENTILATION POSTER

Originally designed to provide ventilation for the sewer systems below the streets, these circular structures are used for advertising.

 I - SPY points: 15

BUSKER

There are often several buskers entertaining passers-by in towns and villages.

 I - SPY points: 15

INFORMATION BOARD

These digital display boards are becoming more popular in towns and are a good way to find out local information.

 I - SPY points: 20

TOURIST INFORMATION

A tourist information office.

 I - SPY points: 10

HÔTEL DE VILLE

Not as you might think, the local hotel, but the town hall.

 I - SPY points: 10

TOWN HALL (MODERN)

Not all the hôtel de ville are old, established buildings. Here is a modern one in the town centre.

 I - SPY points: 15

TOWN PLAN

Many towns have details maps identifying sites and amenities.

 I - SPY points: 15

ELECTRIC CAR

Electric cars are becoming more popular in France. Here is one being charged from a house.

 I - SPY points: 30

FIRE HYDRANT

A modern fire hydrant.

 I - SPY points: 15

WATER PUMP

This old pump would once have been the only source of fresh drinking water for the locals.

 I - SPY points: 25

BOULES

Pétanque or boules, is a game played throughout France on almost any piece of spare land. There are regional differences in the way the game is played.

 I - SPY points: 15

STATUE

This is a statue of Joan of Arc, the Maid of Orleans (1412-1431).

 I - SPY points: 15, for any equestrian statue

STATUE

This is a statue of François Mitterrand, former President of France.

 I - SPY points: 15, for a statue of any individual Frenchman

WAR GRAVES

The fields of northern France were the site of many battles during both World War I and II. There are many war graves commemorating the fallen soldiers of many different countries.

 I - SPY points: 15

WAR MEMORIAL

There are many war memorials around France.

 I - SPY points: 10

BUDGET HOTEL

A convenient and budget priced roadside hotel, very popular in France.

 I - SPY points: 10

HOTEL

A large modern hotel in a city centre.

 I - SPY points: 10

UNIVERSITY

France has many universities and colleges.

 I - SPY points: 10

CHAMPAGNE TOUR

Champagne can only be made in a special area in the north-east region of France. There are some very famous Champagne makers and you can go on a visit of their cellars.

 I - SPY points: 15, double if you go on a cellar tour

Here are some places of entertainment that you may see, or visit.

THEATRE

 I - **SPY** points: 10

MUSEUM

 I - **SPY** points: 10

CINEMA

 I - **SPY** points: 10

Taking a canal boat holiday can be a great way of relaxing and seeing the countryside.

CANAL BOAT

Pleasure boating on a canal.

 I - SPY points: 10

LOCK

Travelling through locks are all part of the fun of a boating holiday.

 I - SPY points: 10

RIVER SIGN

This way to the river.

 I - SPY points: 5

SIGN TO THE CANAL
Canals are well signposted.

I - SPY points: 10

RIVER
Angling is as popular a pastime in France as it is in Britain.

I - SPY points: 10, double if you also see an angler

CHÂTEAU WITH MOAT
To add an additional line of defence, some châteaux have protective moats around them.

I - SPY points: 15

CHÂTEAU

This is a privately owned château. The word château can mean castle, fortress, country seat, mansion, hall or palace.

I - SPY points: 10

CATHEDRAL

You can find a cathedral in most French cities.

I - SPY points: 10

VILLAGE CHURCH

As you travel through France, you will find that most villages, no matter how small, have their own churches.

I - SPY points: 10

VIADUCT

This magnificent arched viaduct dates from the Roman period.

I - SPY points: 20, for any viaduct

WINDMILL

Windmills use the breeze to turn their sails.

 I - SPY points: 15

WIND TURBINE

Wine turbines use the wind to generate electricity.

 I - SPY points: 15

49

WALLED CITY

There would have been many walled cities in medieval France. A handful still exist, their remaining walls are an imposing barrier.

 I - SPY points: 25

ARCHAEOLOGICAL SITE

There are many important archaeological sites all over France, many dating back to Roman times.

 I - SPY points: 25

In France the law is enforced by both the Police, their vehicles are easily identifiable by red stripes and blue lettering on a white background and by Gendarmes, with their blue vehicles.

POLICE PATROL CAR

 I - SPY points: 10

POLICE VAN

 I - SPY points: 15

POLICE STATION

If you need to find the Gendarmerie, the barracks for the armed police, follow the sign.

 I - SPY points: 15

FIRE ENGINES

The fire appliances used by the Sapeurs-Pompiers, France's fire fighters.

 I - SPY points: 15

AMBULANCE

In case of serious illness or injury, call one of the ambulance services.

 I - SPY points: 15

POLICE MOTORCYCLES

For rapid response, the police use high powered motorcycles.

 I - SPY points: 15

Here are a selection of things that you may find at a service station or garage.

GPL

Some cars have their engines converted so that they can run on Liquefied Petroleum Gas, or GPL.

 I - SPY points: 15

AIR AND WATER

You may need to check on air and water levels.

 I - SPY points: 10

GAS CYLINDERS

Many houses in France do not have a piped gas supply and depend on bottles gas. Garages and supermarkets are the usual source of supply.

 I - SPY points: 15

HARBOUR

Many ports, especially those in the south of France, have glamorous harbours complete with stunning sailing vessels.

 I - SPY points: 15

CLIFFS

Northern France lies on the same lines of geology as southern Britain so it's no surprise that along many parts of France, your first sight of the seaside will be the inland cliffs.

 I - SPY points: 20

LIGHTHOUSE

The lights warn sailors of dangers, such as rocks. Once, most lighthouses were manned by men who had to make sure everything was in working order and that the lights were lit when necessary. Now they are automatic.

 I - SPY points: 15

SANDY BEACH

France has some wonderful sandy beaches and are a great holiday attraction for people from many different countries.

I - SPY points: 15

BEACH UMBRELLAS

It can get very hot at the beach, especially in the south of France and any shade is often at a premium.

I - SPY points: 15

TELESCOPE

You'll often find these telescopes at the seaside. You put a coin in the slot and the telescope works until your time runs out.

I - SPY points: 15

PONT DU NORMANDIE

This is one of the longest cable stay bridges in the world and is located close to Le Havre. Its total length is 2,143m (7,032ft).

 I - SPY points: 25

LE VIADUC DE MILLAU

Another cable stayed road bridge, the Millau Viaduct is the tallest bridge in the world – the summit of one of the masts is 343m (1,125ft) and was opened in 2004.

 I - SPY points: 30

PONT SAINT-BÉNEZET

Also known as the Pont d'Avignon, this medieval bridge was built between 1171 – 1185. Most of it was swept away in a huge flood in 1668. Only four of the original 22 arches survive.

 I - SPY points: 25

HOT AIR BALLOONS

Hot air balloons can often be seen hovering over the countryside on warm days.

 I - SPY points: 20

POWER CABLES

France certainly has some unusually shaped electricity pylons!

 I - SPY points: 15

POWER STATION

Giant concrete cooling towers puff out clouds of steam from power stations.

 I - SPY points: 20

OAK

Oak trees provide very strong timbers and are traditionally used in ship building.

 I - SPY points: 10

PLANE TREE

Narrow country roads are often lined with plane trees.

 I - SPY points: 10

POPLAR

Poplar trees are often planted in rows along roadsides in France.

 I - SPY points: 10

FIR TREE

Tall fir trees are often found in woods and forests.

 I - SPY points: 10

WEEPING WILLOW
Native to China, the Weeping Willow can survive almost anywhere, growing best in moist environments.

 I - SPY points: 15

CHERRY TREE
Cherry trees have been recorded in France since the Bronze age period.

 I - SPY points: 15

SILVER BIRCH
Associated with the start of new life due to its ability to colonise bare land after a forest is felled.

 I - SPY points: 15

OLIVE TREE
Olive trees were introduced to France 2,500 years ago. You'll find them mostly in Provence and the south of France.

 I - SPY points: 15

PIGEON

Just as in Britain, you will find pigeons flocking in town and city centres.

 I - SPY points: 5

MAGPIE

A large black-and-white bird with a long tail. You will often see them feeding on road kill.

 I - SPY points: 10

CROW

The small mountain crow, the Alpine Chough is found in the high peaks of the Alps, Pyrenees and in the Corsica mountains.

 I - SPY points: 20

SPARROW

Can be seen dust bathing at the side of the road or scavenging for crumbs at cafes and town centres.

 I - SPY points: 10

BLACKBIRD

The male blackbird has shiny black plumage, yellow beak and yellow ring around his eye; the female is a dull brown colour.

 I - SPY points: 10

COMMON GULL

You will see gulls abundant in all coastal regions.

 I - SPY points: 5

DUCK

There are many breeds of duck found throughout France.

 I - SPY points: 10

HUMMINGBIRD

Known as Sphinx Colibri, these stunning little creatures, found in the south of France, are actually moths!

 I - SPY points: 35

Even through you have travelled abroad to a different country, there is plenty of evidence of the British at work in France. Here are just a few examples.

I - SPY points: 15, for each of these and any other familiar shops or names you find in France!

HSBC BANK

BARCLAYS BANK

THOMAS COOK

Index

First published by Michelin Maps and Guides 2011 ©
Michelin, Proprietaires-Editeurs 2011. Michelin and the
Michelin Man are registered Trademarks of Michelin.
Created and produced by Blue Sky Publishing Limited.
All rights reserved. No part of this publication may be
reproduced, copied or transmitted in any form without
the prior consent of the publisher.
Print services by FingerPrint International Book
production – fingerprint@pandora.be. The publisher
gratefully acknowledges the contribution of the I-Spy
team: Camilla Lovell, Geoff Watts and Jordan Watts in
the production of this title.
The publisher gratefully acknowledges the contribution
of Robert Lorges, Romain Monin, Elena Ibanes, Frederic
Blanc, Isabelle Parant and Unitaw Limited who provided
the photographs in this book.
Other images in the public domain and under a
creative commons licence. All logos, images, designs
and image rights are © the copyright holders and are
used with kind thanks and permission.
Reprinted 2014   10 9 8 7 6 5 4 3 2

I-SPY

One Token

715947

HOW TO GET YOUR
I-SPY CERTIFICATE AND BADGE

Every time you score 1000 points or more in an I-Spy book, you can apply for a certificate

HERE'S WHAT TO DO, STEP BY STEP:

Certificate

- Ask an adult to check your score
- Ask his or her permission to apply for a certificate
- Apply online to www.ispymichelin.com
- Enter your name and address and the completed title
- We will send you back via e mail your certificate for the title

Badge

- Each I-Spy title has a cut out (page corner) token at the back of the book
- Collect five tokens from different I-Spy titles
- Put Second Class Stamps on two strong envelopes
- Write your own address on one envelope and put a £1 coin inside it (for protection). Fold, but do not seal the envelope, and place it inside the second envelope
- Write the following address on the second envelope, seal it carefully and post to:

I-Spy Books
Michelin Maps and Guides
Hannay House
39 Clarendon Road
Watford
WD17 1JA